PRAISE FOR **HAND TO GOD**

"The freshest and funniest Broadway comedy in years . . . *Hand to God* is to plays as *The Book of Mormon* is to musicals . . . it entertains the devil out of you." —ADAM FELDMAN, *Time Out NY*

"Mr. Askins's black comedy about the divided human soul stands out . . . merry and scary and very welcome." —CHARLES ISHERWOOD, *The New York Times*

"An irresistible, intelligent, heartbreaking blood-dark comedy, it's as disturbing as it is funny, vile as it is violent and, to my mind, better for both." —JESSE GREEN, *New York* magazine

"The Broadway comedy *Hand to God* is so ridiculously raunchy, irreverent, and funny, it's bound to leave you sore from laughing. Ah, hurts so good. Askins proves deft at writing dialogue that's hysterical and at serving insights about organised religion and family discussion." —JOE DZIEMIANOWICZ, *New York Daily News*

"As touching as it is screamingly funny . . . Askins's most impressive talent, though is his ability to make us laugh while juggling those big themes that make life so terrifying: death, depression, alcoholism, sexual guilt, emotional repression, religious hypocrisy and the eternal battle between your good puppet and your bad puppet." —MARILYN STASIO, *Variety*

"Darkly funny . . . Askins is clearly interested in exploring the psychology of grief, repression of human nature and adolescent unease on his own unconventional terms, while also making what for many will be quite provocative statements about the moral ambiguities of Christianity. —DAVID ROONEY, *The Hollywood Reporter*

"Askins provides a series of beautifully sculpted scenes that intensify in danger. Arguably the best play of the Broadway season." —DAVID FINKLE, *Huffington Post*

ROBERT ASKINS's *Hand to God* opened on Broadway in April 2015, following two critically-acclaimed off-Broadway runs, where it was named a *New York Times* Critics' Pick and called "the most entertaining show of 2014." His plays include *The Squirrels*, *The Carpenter*, and *Permission,* which had its world premiere off-Broadway at MCC Theater. He has received two EST/Sloan grants, the Helen Merrill Emerging Playwrights Award, and an Arch and Bruce Davis Award for Playwriting. Rob is an I-73 and Youngblood alum and a graduate of Baylor University.

HAND TO GOD

A Play by

ROBERT ASKINS

THE OVERLOOK PRESS
NEW YORK, NY

This edition first published in the United States in 2018 by
The Overlook Press, Peter Mayer Publishers, Inc.

141 Wooster Street
New York, NY 10012
www.overlookpress.com
For bulk and special sales, please contact sales@overlookpress.com,
or write to us at the address above.

Cataloging-in-Publication Data is available from the Library of Congress

Book design and type formatting by Bernard Schleifer
Manufactured in the United States of America
ISBN 978-1-4683-1392-5
1 3 5 7 9 10 8 6 4 2

This play is for my father

TO THE READER OF THIS PLAY

Hi! Hello! How are you?

My name is Rob Askins and I wrote the play you're holding in your hands and if you are holding this script I would like to say congratulations. The play section is usually very small and hard to find. It's always in some corner next to poetry or maybe books about music or graphic novels or whatever.

So if you're reading these words then it isn't by accident. You must have heard something about this thing. You must have sought it out or ordered it online and now you are here reading the foreword. So odds are you're a "theatre person" and not just any "theatre person," you're a "theatre nerd."

So congratulations nerd this, now, is your play.

I wrote it but you now have a copy, which means you can make it. You can't charge money for the ticket or my agent will get very angry and that's a whole thing, so don't, but you can now make this play, even if it's just in your head.

So now it's our play and I want you to know I take that very seriously.

When I was 22 living in Texas and bartending and writing plays and dreaming about New York, I would go to the bookstore and pick up the scripts for plays that had won things and I would sit in the aisle and read them all day. I remember reading a very famous play that won everything and looking up when I finished it and going "Really? That's it?"

That's the funny thing about what you have in your hands. This is a blueprint. It is a suggestion. It is a speech bubble in a long conversation. It is an invitation to play.

So to prepare you to make this play here are some things I would like you to know.

1. Puppet ministries are real. My mother ran one. I was in it. Go on-line Google it real quick. You'll see. A couple hundred dollars and a dream and you too can have your own.

2. The puppet I had never talked to me. It never bit off anybody's ear and my mother never had sex with a teen (that I know of), but my father did die and I had a hard time with that. So take our play seriously but know there are jokes here.

3. Chicken fried steak has no chicken in it, but it is delicious and you should try it if you get the chance. It is the national dish of Texas. This play is about Texas and the people who live there. Like chicken fried steak we are strange and delicious and if you get us right some things in our play will be easier to understand.

4. Read Tyrone in a funny voice. It will help. If you are not funny have a funny friend read it. If you are funny look in a mirror and say the lines. That will help you get a better understanding of this play.

5. I love these people and if our play is going to be any good you should love them too. They are trying very hard. The play will not be good if you make fun of them. Try to understand them. They are in pain. Just like you.

6. Our play is big. When people feel they feel all the way. When they cry they scream. When they love they hit. This might not make sense to some people, but other people will know what I'm talking about. If you don't get it give it the benefit of the doubt. You might have a different kind of family.

7. This play does not hate God. It does not hate church or Jesus. It is frustrated by them. It wants them to be better. It wants people to be better and if it hates anything it hates easy answers and people who have stopped looking.

8. Scare your audience. Try to turn them on. Make them laugh. Make them cry. Make them scream. Go for the jugular. BITE

THEM. MAKE THEM EAT PAPER. IN THE THEATRE YOU CAN DO ANYTHING, SO DO EVERYTHING. This applies even if you are the only member of the audience.

I hope you like our play. I hope it makes you laugh. I hope it makes you feel something. I hope it makes you want to make plays and if you already make them make them different and make them weird because I would like to see more good weird plays.

This play is what it looks like in my head. I would like to see what it looks like inside yours.

Good luck.

Robert Askins

HAND TO GOD

Hand to God was developed by the Ensemble Studio Theatre/ Young-blood Program at Southampton Arts in July 2011 and received its world premiere production at the Ensemble Studio Theatre (William Carden, Artistic Director; Paul Alexander Slee, Executive Director) in October 2011. It was directed by Moritz von Stuelpnagel; the set design was by Rebecca Lord-Surratt; the costume design was by Sydney Maresca; the lighting design was by Matthew Richards; the sound design was by Chris Barlow; the puppet design was by Marte Johanne Ekhougen; the fight director was Robert Westley; and the production stage manager was Michele Ebel. The cast was as follows:

JASON/TYRONE	Steven Boyer
MARGERY	Geneva Carr
PASTOR GREG	Scott Sowers
TIMMY	Bobby Moreno
JESSICA	Megan Hill

The Off-Broadway premiere of *Hand to God* was presented by MCC Theater (Robert LuPone, Bernard Telsey & William Cantler, Artistic Directors; Blake West, Executive Director) on March 10, 2014. It was directed by Moritz von Stuelpnagel; the set design was by Beowulf Boritt; the costume design was by Sydney Maresca; the lighting design was by Jason Lyons; the sound design was by Jill BC DuBoff; the puppet design was by Marte Johanne Ekhougen; the fight director was Robert Westley; and the production manager was B. D. White. The cast was as follows:

JASON/TYRONE	Steven Boyer
MARGERY	Geneva Carr
PASTOR GREG	Marc Kudisch
TIMMY	Michael Oberholtzer
JESSICA	Sarah Stiles

PROLOGUE

All is dark.

Then a light.

Then a PUPPET *into the light.*

The PUPPET *is cute, cuddly. You've seen something like this before.*

I mean he looks Elmo-y and shit, but as he goes on you can tell there's something wrong with him.

He's weirder.

Darker.

Whatever . . .

TYRONE In the beginning there was no divide. We were too stupid to be anything but what we were. We didn't shave. We rutted as we chose careless in the night. When you had to shit . . . you just let it drop. It was a golden age. Then some evil bastard figured out many together could kill larger things. Then the ladies figured out if you have more food from larger things less babies die. So we started camping. Together. That's where the trouble started. All of a sudden you couldn't just rut or shit or stare off for long periods of time. If some other took to your lady. He didn't just kill you or you him. Other things had to happen. To preserve the group. And some asshole. Probably the same one that figured out how to kill really big things in groups. He invented right and wrong. Right is for all of us. Wrong is for just you. Peace around the camp fire.

Good. You shitting in the middle of the sleeping place bad. Preservation of numbers good. Stoning to death the guy with the really high voice that won't shut the fuck up in his sleep, bad. Families and babies and more and more, good. Extracurricular fucking, bad . . . but unavoidable. So the same mutherfucker who invented the group kill and team virtue, that ballsy piece of pig shit topped all his previous work and he invented . . . The devil. When I have put myself ahead of the group. When I have acted badly, in order that I may stay around the camp fire all I have to do is say . . . The devil made me do it.

The PUPPET *laughs.*

ACT 1. SCENE 1.

The lights come up on the basement of a church.

The basement of a church in Texas.

The basement of a church in Cypress, Texas.

There are posters. One has a rainbow of children holding hands and running toward a white bearded Christ.

There is a brightly colored rug. There are bean bag chairs.

There are four people in the room. One grown-up and three kids.

The kids are played by actors that look young. But by no means the 15-17-year-olds that they are intended to be.

MARGERY *is standing in the middle of the room. She has a primish looking lady puppet on her hand.*

MARGERY Hey y'all my name's Rita and I love Jesus! Do you love Jesus?

She laughs to herself. Enjoying her puppet voice.

But then she looks around the room.

Nobody seems to love Jesus.

Nobody seems to want to be there.

The boys are JASON *and* TIMOTHY.

The girl is JESSICA.

JASON *is blond and slight and slightly afraid.*

TIMOTHY *is in all black.*

JESSICA *is dark haired and thin.*

JESSICA *is working on her puppet a little hunched over in the corner.*

MARGERY   Well where's everybody at? Jessie you gonna finish your . . .

JESSICA   Jolene.

MARGERY   You gonna finish Jolene today.

JESSICA   I guess.

JESSICA *pulls a load of stuffing out of the puppet supply bag.*

She maybe starts stuffing it under the puppet's shirt.

MARGERY   Whoa Jessie how much of that stuffing do you need?

JESSICA   You said I could make her look like I wanted.

MARGERY   Yes but what is all that for.

TIMOTHY   Puppet boobs.

JESSICA   Shut up Timothy.

TIMOTHY   It's not my fault you got no tits.

MARGERY   Hello Tim.

JASON   (*To* JESSICA.) I think you look nice.

JESSICA   Umm thanks.

TIMOTHY   Dude I can see your boner from here.

MARGERY   Stop it Tim, that is enough.

TIMOTHY   What? I'm the one that's being forced to look at a boner. I'm the victim here.

MARGERY   Timothy, you cannot see his boner.

JASON   Mom.

MARGERY   Timothy. Tim . . . T . . . do you even have your puppet Timothy.

TIMOTHY   Uhhh. No.

MARGERY   Why don't you have a puppet, Timothy.

TIMOTHY 'Cause puppet are for faggots.

MARGERY Timothy.

JESSICA You are so . . .

TIMOTHY What?

JESSICA Afraid.

MARGERY Jessica.

TIMOTHY Afraid of what?

JESSICA *Afraid you're gay.*

MARGERY Hey now.

TIMOTHY What?

JESSICA That's why you say that.

TIMOTHY See if you can taste the gay when I nut in your mouth.

MARGERY Timothy behave.

TIMOTHY Or what?

MARGERY Or I'll tell your Mother.

TIMOTHY If you can get her when she's sober.

(Beat.)

MARGERY Kids this can be really great. Really rewarding if you just . . . just . . .

TIMOTHY Just what.

MARGERY Just took it seriously. Hey show them what you've been working on.

JASON Mooooommmmm.

MARGERY It's cool it's really, cool. Rad even.

JASON Please Mom don't say rad.

MARGERY Why not?

JESSICA Yeah why not? She can say rad.

MARGERY I can say rad.

TIMOTHY You can totally say rad. Mrs. S.

MARGERY See Jason. So now go ahead. Show them. Show them what you been working on.

JASON *stands and brings up his puppet,* TYRONE *and starts a very faint and very self-conscious rendition of "Jesus Loves Me."*

He is not a bad puppeteer but he isn't selling it.

JASON Jesus loves me this I know, for the Bible tells me so.

Continuing over the chatter.

TIMOTHY Jesus loves you in your butt hole.

JESSICA You're so far back in the closet, you're in Narnia.

TIMOTHY What?

MARGERY QUIET.

JASON *continues.*

MARGERY Why are you two here?

JESSICA Well really I'm more into Balinese shadow puppetry, but I'll take what I can get.

TIMOTHY 'Cause Mom won't leave me at home during her meetings.

JESSICA What meetings.

TIMOTHY None of your business you nosy bitch.

MARGERY TIMOTHY. You can't . . . that is . . .

JASON'*s still going.*

MARGERY Jason that's enough.

JASON *keeps going.*

MARGERY Jason.

And going.

MARGERY Baby stop.

JASON Sorry Mom.

MARGERY *pauses. She hangs her head.*

MARGERY   Jason. Jessica. Will you leave me and Timothy alone?

JASON   Mom.

MARGERY   Just for a second, baby.

TIMOTHY   Awww. Little baby.

MARGERY   Shut up, Timothy.

(*Beat.*)

MARGERY   I'm . . . I . . .

JESSICA   Jason you wanna get a coke? I know where Pastor Greg keeps them.

JASON *looks at* TIMOTHY *and his mother.*

JASON   Okay.

They exit.

TIMOTHY *and* MARGERY *are left alone on stage.*

MARGERY   Do you hate me Timothy?

TIMOTHY   (*Suddenly quiet.*) No.

MARGERY   I cain't keep doing this Tim. It is every week. Every week. I have had a hard year. I have had a hard year.

TIMOTHY *doesn't say anything.*

MARGERY   I have one thing in my life that is keeping me together and that is my dedication to my lord and savior Jesus Christ and because I can't sing and I can't preach and my brownies taste like old tires I am trying to teach myself and you how to do puppet shows. Now if you don't want to come here you don't have to come here. Go smoke in the parking lot and I will tell your mother you are in here. But please leave me alone. I beg you to leave me alone.

She hangs her head.

TIMOTHY Why are you sad?

MARGERY My husband died.

TIMOTHY How?

MARGERY He . . . he . . . he . . .

TIMOTHY I mean, I know he had a heart attack.

MARGERY Then why did you ask?

TIMOTHY 'Cause I want you to know I care.

MARGERY Then why won't you leave me alone?

TIMOTHY 'Cause I love you and I don't know what to do about it.

MARGERY Excuse me.

TIMOTHY Should I say it again.

MARGERY No Timothy. You shouldn't. You shouldn't ever say that again.

TIMOTHY Why not.

MARGERY Because . . . because . . .

TIMOTHY Because you feel it too?

MARGERY No. No Timothy. No.

TIMOTHY I . . . I love our little talks.

MARGERY Little ta . . .? I am disciplining you.

TIMOTHY I thought this was our thing.

MARGERY Do what now?

TIMOTHY You remember when we was alone that one time Jason was sick and Jessica's family was in Florida and we had a great talk and I made you laugh and you touched my arm and then the room got hot and I don't know much but I know when I'm hard . . .

MARGERY (*Calling off stage.*) Jason.

TIMOTHY And I'm rocking a halfsie right now, so . . .

MARGERY What you felt wasn't what I felt.

TIMOTHY Okay. Then don't kiss me.

MARGERY Fine.

He steps toward her.

MARGERY Timothy.

TIMOTHY Just don't kiss me.

He steps toward her again.

MARGERY Stop it.

TIMOTHY Don't do it.

He is getting close.

MARGERY This is a stupid game.

He is so close she has to move.

TIMOTHY Then why are you moving?

MARGERY Because you're making me uncomfortable.

TIMOTHY Oh.

This has the desired effect.

TIMOTHY I'm sorry. I thought . . .

MARGERY That's fine. Just . . . I don't think you should come to puppet practice anymore.

TIMOTHY Why?

MARGERY You don't want to learn. You're disruptive and you make me uncomfortable.

TIMOTHY But that . . . that would hurt too much.

The door opens.

PASTOR GREG *walks in.*

PASTOR GREG Knock. Knock. Knock.

He's a nice guy. In slacks.

No collar. A brisk walk.

PASTOR GREG Over so soon.

MARGERY We were just . . .

TIMOTHY I was just leaving.

PASTOR GREG Have a blessed day.

TIMOTHY *flips him the bird as he makes his exit.*

PASTOR GREG Troubled kid.

MARGERY Yeah.

PASTOR GREG How was puppet practice today?

MARGERY It was . . . I am daily being taught lessons of patience and forgiveness.

PASTOR GREG Thatta girl. When can we expect the debut of your Christcateers?

MARGERY I don't know, Pastor Greg.

PASTOR GREG Will giving you a deadline help?

MARGERY I don't think so.

PASTOR GREG Well I do. Service, next Sunday yer on the bill and if you don't have a presentation it'll be up to you to explain it.

MARGERY But . . .

PASTOR GREG Ah ah ah no buts. The church has been more than generous with space and resources . . .

MARGERY Fine. I'll see what I can do.

PASTOR GREG Thatta girl.

MARGERY *packs up her puppet and her Bible.*

PASTOR GREG There's also gonna be a potluck after.

MARGERY Oh.

PASTOR GREG Yeah.

MARGERY Huh.

PASTOR GREG Will you be there.

MARGERY I wasn't plannin on . . .

PASTOR GREG I would sure like it if you came.

MARGERY   Oh Pastor Greg.

PASTOR GREG   I know you don't get on well with the ladies auxiliary, but I think these puppets are gonna be a big hit.

MARGERY   Oh Pastor Greg.

PASTOR GREG   And I promise I will not leave your side.

MARGERY   Oh Pastor Greg.

PASTOR GREG   Try me you'll like me.

PASTOR GREG   Least gimme a "we'll see"?

MARGERY   It hasn't been but six months . . .

PASTOR GREG   Just a "we'll see".

MARGERY   (*Sigh.*) We'll see.

PASTOR GREG   Great. I'll see you there. You have a blessed day.

MARGERY   Night Pastor.

ACT 1. SCENE 2.

So in time we are a little after JESSICA *and* JASON *left the basement.*

They're sitting on playground swings. Drinking coke from cans.

JESSICA *has taken her puppet off.*

JASON *has not.*

JASON *takes a drink of his soda.*

He is using the puppet mouth to hold the can.

It's a little funny.

JESSICA *maybe giggles.*

JASON *maybe gets red.*

Maybe switches the soda to his other hand.

JESSICA You don't take that thing off much do you?

JASON I do. I do all the time. I spend long periods of time with it off. Like in the bath. Or when swimming. Or . . .

JESSICA Only when dealing with water.

JASON What?

JESSICA What, is he some kinda hydrophobe?

JASON Who Tyrone?

JESSICA Is that his name?

JASON Ummm. Yeah.

JESSICA And he's afraid of water.

JASON I know what hydrophobe means.

JESSICA I didn't think you didn't.

JASON He just takes a really long time to dry. You take him into the pool once and there goes your Saturday night, alone in the bathroom with the hair dryer.

She giggles again.

He gets red again.

JESSICA Aww you're embarrassed.

JASON I'm not embarrassed.

JESSICA You don't have to be embarrassed.

JASON Good I'm not.

JESSICA I think it's sweet how much you love your puppet.

JASON I don't love my puppet.

JESSICA Well how much you like your puppet.

JASON I don't like my puppet.

JESSICA How much you need your puppet.

He gets up to go.

JESSICA Hey. Hey, don't leave.

JASON Stop making fun of me.

JESSICA I'm not.

JASON I'm . . .

JESSICA Really I'm not. I saw *The Lion King*. I think it's cool.

JASON Are you sure you're not making fun of me.

JESSICA I'm sure.

JASON 'Cause I know it's not cool.

JESSICA It is.

JASON You don't have to patronize me.

JESSICA I'm not. I like it when you make him sing.

This one lets him believe her.

JASON Thank you.

He turns around.

JASON You wanna see something.

JESSICA Ummm.

JASON You'll like it.

JESSICA Yeah?

JASON I think you'll like it.

JESSICA Okay.

JASON Okay.

JASON *slicks back his hair. Takes a deep breath and then says . . .*

JASON Well Costello, I'm goin to New York with you. You know
   Buck Harris the Yankee's manager gave me a job as coach as
   long as you're on the team.

TYRONE Look Abbott, if you're the coach, you must know all the
   players.

JASON I certainly do.

TYRONE Well I've never met the guys. So you'll have to tell me their
   names and then I'll know who's playing on the team.

JASON Oh I'll tell you their names, but you know it seems to me they
   give these ball players now-a-days very particular names.

*As he starts he's a little aspergersy, but as he goes on he gets
more and more comfortable.*

TYRONE You mean funny names?

JASON Well let's see we have on the bags, Who's on first, What's
   on second, I don't know is on third . . .

TYRONE That's what I want to find out.

JASON I say Who's on first, What's on second, I don't know's on
   third.

TYRONE Are you the manager?

JASON Yes.

TYRONE You gonna be the coach too?

JASON Yes.

TYRONE And you don't know the fellows' names.

JASON Well I should.

TYRONE Then who's on first?

JASON Yes?

TYRONE I mean the fellow's name.

JASON Who.

TYRONE The guy on first.

JASON Who.

TYRONE The first baseman.

JASON Who.

TYRONE The guy playing . . .

JASON *is really into it. You can imagine him going into it all alone on a Saturday night.*

JESSICA *is giggling a bit.*

JASON Who is on first.

TYRONE I'm askin you who's on first.

JASON That's the man's name.

TYRONE That's whose name.

JASON Yes.

TYRONE Well go ahead and tell me.

JASON I just did.

TYRONE Who?

JASON Yes.

JASON *reaches a pause in the routine and looks out at her.*

He becomes aware of what he's doing.

JESSICA What are you doing. Don't stop.

JASON I . . .

He gets red.

JESSICA What?

JASON I can't remember anymore.

JESSICA That's really good.

JASON Thank you.

JASON *goes back to sit down.*

JESSICA Did you come up with that all by yourself.

JASON Yes.

TYRONE (*As if on his own.*) Liar.

JASON *grabs one hand with the other.*

JASON Shut up.

JESSICA *giggles.*

TYRONE *wriggles free.*

TYRONE It's a famous routine from the fifties.

JASON Thirties.

TYRONE You'd know that if you weren't so stupid.

JESSICA Hey.

JASON Shut up Tyrone.

JESSICA Yeah, shut up Tyrone.

TYRONE But it doesn't matter 'cause he thinks you're hot.

JASON That is enough.

JASON *puts his hand over the* PUPPET'*s mouth.*

JESSICA You think I'm hot.

JASON No . . .

She looks a little hurt.

JASON Yes.

She looks a little embarrassed.

JASON I don't know.

The PUPPET *bites* JASON*'s finger.*

JASON *puts his finger in his mouth.*

JASON Ouch.

TYRONE So hot. So hot he can't keep from touching himself.

JESSICA Jason.

TYRONE Touching himself in the dark.

JESSICA Jason stop.

JASON Tyrone.

TYRONE The things he thinks about you.

JESSICA Jason this isn't funny.

JASON I know.

TYRONE Thinks about doing to you.

JASON Tyrone.

TYRONE What.

JASON Stop.

TYRONE You can't stop it.

JASON Yes I can.

JASON *grabs the* PUPPET *by the neck in a violent motion and pulls it clear off.*

He throws it to the ground.

There is of course a pause.

JASON Jessica. I . . .

JESSICA I'm gonna see if my dad's here.

JASON I'm sorry.

JESSICA It's okay. It's fine. Don't even worry.

JASON Don't go.

JESSICA   I'll see you next week.

JASON   Please don't go.

JESSICA   Bye now.

JESSICA *goes.* JASON *watches her go.*

He goes over to the PUPPET.

He takes the PUPPET *up and holds it by the sides of the head.*

JASON   Shit.

ACT 1. SCENE 3.

MARGERY and JASON are in the car. Amy Grant or some other mid-nineties Christian pop singer is playing.

JASON is staring out his window sucking on his finger.

The PUPPET is on his lap.

MARGERY is driving straight ahead.

MARGERY What do you want for dinner?

JASON doesn't answer.

MARGERY Chick-fil-A? You want some nuggets. Some chicken nuggets?

JASON doesn't answer.

MARGERY You hungry? You really . . . we could go to Grandy's. They got that Chicken Fried Steak you like.

JASON looks at her.

JASON Momma. I don't wanna do the puppets no more.

MARGERY swallows hard.

MARGERY TCBY.

JASON Momma did you hear me.

MARGERY Get you a parfait.

JASON I cain't. I cain't do it no more.

MARGERY That's what we'll do. We'll get you a parfait. Parfait means perfect in French.

JASON Momma . . .

MARGERY You can keep on repeating yourself, young man. I'm
gonna keep on ignoring you.

JASON Why, Momma.

MARGERY You know what them puppets mean to your Momma.

JASON I do.

MARGERY You know Momma's having a rough time right now.

JASON I do.

MARGERY You know Momma needs your help.

JASON I know but . . .

MARGERY But what?

JASON I cain't. I . . .

MARGERY What is more important than your Momma's love?

JASON I think it's doing bad things to me.

MARGERY What are you talking about.

JASON Just please Momma. Lemme stop and don't think it means
nothing.

MARGERY Jason we gotta perform for the church next Sunday.

JASON No Momma.

MARGERY I was gonna tell you over chicken nuggets but there.
There it is. We gonna have to give 'em a show next week and
I need you to go up there and show 'em. Show 'em what you
can do. You and ole Tyrone.

JASON I don't think Tyrone'll like that.

MARGERY Jason what have I told you about that kinna talk.

JASON Not to talk it.

MARGERY When you talk about Tyrone wanting things it . . .

JASON Yes Ma'am.

MARGERY So. I need you to practice extra hard this week. Work on
your church songs. You're the only one who's any good. Cut it out

with that old vaudeville mess and come through for Momma.
Can you? Can you come through for Momma?

She pauses.

She waits.

MARGERY Can you be her rock.

She waits.

MARGERY Her knight in shining armor.

She waits.

MARGERY Please.

JASON No Momma.

MARGERY Yes Jason.

JASON I won't do it.

MARGERY Jason.

JASON I won't.

MARGERY You will.

JASON You can't make me.

MARGERY I am your mother and I can.

JASON It's bad.

MARGERY I'll tell you what's bad.

JASON Oh yeah.

MARGERY Yeah.

JASON Oh yeah.

MARGERY Yeah.

JASON What about this.

JASON *rips the* PUPPET*'s head in half.*

MARGERY *gasps, her eyes go wide.*

She slams on the brakes.

MARGERY Get out.

JASON What.

MARGERY Get out of the car.

JASON Momma.

MARGERY Get out of the car you spoiled little shit. Get out of the car. Get out of the car get out of the car.

JASON No Momma.

MARGERY Now.

JASON Momma. Please.

MARGERY Do it.

JASON Momma I love you.

MARGERY No you don't.

JASON I do. I do.

MARGERY No you. None of you do.

JASON Momma.

She screams.

JASON Momma.

She screams again.

JASON Momma I miss Dad too.

He tries to touch her.

MARGERY Don't say it. Don't say anything. Just go.

JASON *gets out of the car.*

There's a tire screech and MARGERY *wheels off.*

JASON *starts the long walk home.*

ACT 1. SCENE 4.

We're in the basement.

MARGERY *is sitting down behind a desk like a teacher.*

PASTOR GREG *is sitting on the desk facing her.*

MARGERY They're not here.

PASTOR GREG I can see that.

MARGERY They're not here, and they're not coming.

PASTOR GREG Margery . . .

MARGERY I don't know what kind of performance we can have without any of the performers.

PASTOR GREG The Lord works in mysterious ways.

MARGERY I don't know what to do.

PASTOR GREG Stop trying to do.

MARGERY What does that mean.

PASTOR GREG Just be still.

MARGERY I cain't.

PASTOR GREG Give me your hands.

MARGERY Pastor.

PASTOR GREG Just give 'em to me.

She does.

PASTOR GREG Close your eyes.

MARGERY I . . .

PASTOR GREG Please.

She does.

PASTOR GREG Breathe deep.

She does.

He starts to rub her hands.

PASTOR GREG Let it all go. Think how small our lives
are in the bigness of the universe. Feel how tiny we are in the
palm of God's hand. Feel supported by Him. Think how easy it
is to live. Breathe. Be. Think about how little energy this takes.
Make your mind as empty as you can. Make your world as
simple as you can. Try to bring yourself to a place of surrender.
Open your eyes . . .

She does.

PASTOR GREG And just see what's right in front of you.

The PASTOR *is smiling a little too big.*

MARGERY *jolts up and drops his hands.*

MARGERY Oh God.

PASTOR GREG Yes well.

MARGERY I'm sorry Pastor. I'm not . . .

PASTOR GREG What?

MARGERY Nothing.

PASTOR GREG No you started.

MARGERY I'm not ready.

PASTOR GREG Ready for what?

MARGERY I am not interested . . . in you.

PASTOR GREG Oh. I . . .

MARGERY I think you're wonderful. Sweet. Gentle. Good. I think you're a good man.

PASTOR GREG   But you're not in the market for good?

MARGERY   I'm just not in the market. I lost my husband and I don't know who I am anymore.

PASTOR GREG   I know. I know you're a wounded thing that needs to be cared for. I know you need for someone to share your burden. You need someone to pull in harness with you. I know what empty days are like Margery. I know what lonely nights are like. I know what it's like when you eat your lunch in silence and you think you're choking down dry white bread and then you realize it's half a cry. I know what it's like to look at your arms and ask what use are these empty. I know what it's like to wanna scream at happy couples on the street just 'cause they're happy. Just cause they're together and you're not. I'm not the biggest man in the world Margery. I'm not so rich or so handsome or so . . . good. I am not so good. But I got empty arms. Empty arms and ears made just to hear you cry. That's my best shot Margery. I think we could be good together, real and whole, and if you think there's even a sliver of a section of a portion of a chance I wish you'd give it to me. 'Cause I sure could use a break.

MARGERY   No Pastor I don't think that there is.

PASTOR GREG   Oh. Okay.

She reaches out to him he pulls back real hard.

PASTOR GREG   Please no. Not now.

He clouds up.

PASTOR GREG   I'ma go.

MARGERY   But what about Sunday?

PASTOR GREG   You'll figure something out Margery.

He makes for the door.

MARGERY Pastor.

PASTOR GREG I hope you find what you're looking for.

He leaves.

She stares after him.

Hangs her head.

She puts her hands on the sides of her desk.

Her fingers curl into a fist.

She picks the desk a up a little off the ground.

She slams it back down.

She pulls a desk drawer right the fuck out.

Its contents spill out all over the floor.

She takes the chair she's been sitting on. She holds it over her head.

Just then . . .

TIMOTHY *comes on.*

MARGERY ARRRG.

TIMOTHY I found my puppet.

MARGERY *throws the chair.*

TIMOTHY Cool.

MARGERY Go home Timothy.

TIMOTHY No way. If we're breaking shit. I'm staying.

He kicks over a chair.

TIMOTHY Yeah. Take that chair.

MARGERY Please Timothy.

TIMOTHY Just tell me what you want me to break. I'll break it.

MARGERY That's stupid.

TIMOTHY That bookshelf. I'll break that bookshelf.

TIMOTHY *puts his foot through the middle of the cheap plastic shelf.*

TIMOTHY See. I'll break things.

MARGERY I know you'll break things.

TIMOTHY I'll break things for you.

She stares at him.

Stupid and hair triggered.

MARGERY Yeah.

TIMOTHY You know I will.

MARGERY I always hated that poster.

TIMOTHY Which one.

MARGERY The one with all those happy kids singing.

TIMOTHY This one.

MARGERY Yeah. That one.

TIMOTHY What do you want.

MARGERY You know what I want.

TIMOTHY I do, but I want you to say it.

MARGERY You want me to say it.

TIMOTHY Yeah.

MARGERY Yeah.

TIMOTHY Yeah.

MARGERY Break it for me Timmy.

TIMOTHY Yes Ma'am.

TIMOTHY *takes the picture off the wall. He rips it in two.*

MARGERY Yeah rip it up.

Then in four.

TIMOTHY Like that.

MARGERY Yeah. Timmy tear it to pieces.

Then again.

TIMOTHY   You like this.

MARGERY   Smaller and smaller.

Rip.

TIMOTHY   Tell me what you want.

Rippy rip rip.

MARGERY   I want . . .

TIMOTHY   What.

MARGERY   I want . . .

TIMOTHY   Tell me.

Hands fulla pieces.

MARGERY   I want you to eat it.

He doesn't even think.

He just crams the poster into his mouth.

MARGERY   Eat it for me Timmy.

He does.

He crams more and more of the ripped up poster into his mouth.

She starts to walk towards him.

TIMOTHY   (*Through a full mouth.*) Yesh Maaam.

MARGERY   Eat it all for me Tim-Tim.

He gives it a dry swallow.

TIMOTHY   I'm doing my best.

MARGERY   Do better.

He chokes a piece down.

TIMOTHY   Yesh Maaam.

MARGERY You're missing pieces. There and there.

She bends down and picks up a piece of the poster off the ground.

TIM I'm tryin'.

MARGERY Open your mouth.

He does. It is not pretty.

TIMOTHY Ahhhh.

She shoves it in his mouth.

He maybe chokes a little bit.

He steps back.

MARGERY You are one stupid piece of trash ain't you little Tim.

TIMOTHY You're one crazy fucked up bitch ain't you Mrs. Stevens.

MARGERY I been so good for so long and it isn't paying off. Timmy.

TIMOTHY I don't give a shit.

MARGERY Yeah me neither. Kick over that chair.

He does.

TIMOTHY What else.

MARGERY Break that light bulb.

TIMMY *jumps. He knocks into the light fixture. The light goes out.*

TIMOTHY Cool.

MARGERY Rip open my shirt.

TIMOTHY Umm.

(*Beat.*)

MARGERY Quick or I'mma take it back.

He steps up.

He does it.

He looks at her body.

TIMOTHY Hallelujah

MARGERY Bite me Tim.

TIMOTHY Where?

She slaps him.

MARGERY Don't you ask me where. Just pick a fucking spot and
do it.

He does.

She cries out just a little bit.

TIMOTHY I'm sorry.

MARGERY I'll give you something to be sorry about.

She grabs his head.

Pushes it down her body.

He mumbles something.

TIMOTHY Mrs. Stevens.

MARGERY What Tim?

TIMOTHY This is not how I pictured it . . .

She wrenches his head around to look at her.

MARGERY New rules, Tim.

TIMOTHY Yeah.

MARGERY Yeah. One no more talking.

TIMOTHY Okay.

MARGERY NO MORE TALKING. Rule two. Don't be nice.

He kisses her. She pushes him back.

MARGERY Don't be nice.

He comes in again a bit rougher. She pushes him off again.

MARGERY DON'T BE NICE.

She slaps him.

As he reels she socks him, closed fist.

Timmy loses it.

He grabs her roughly.

Maybe he chokes her.

Maybe he sinks his teeth into her neck.

Whatever happens.

She screams hard.

He pulls out to check in.

She laughs crazy and kisses him.

And they're back in it.

With everything they've got.

ACT 1. SCENE 5.

A bed rolls on.

JASON *is in it.*

Unbeknownst to JASON.

TYRONE *is very much awake.*

TYRONE *has repaired himself.*

He is tougher looking now.

He stares at JASON *while* JASON *sleeps.*

TYRONE   Wake up.

The PUPPET *spits on* JASON.

JASON *wipes his eyes awake.*

JASON   Huh. Wha.

TYRONE   You pull some shit like that again. I'll cut off your balls.

JASON   Tyrone . . . how'd you get. . . .

TYRONE   Better. How'd I get fixed. I didn't whine and ask questions
I just got that shit done.

JASON   I'm glad you're feeling better.

TYRONE   You don't want me better you want me dead.

JASON   No Tyrone.

TYRONE   You tore my goddamn head in two.

JASON   You called me out in front of Jessica.

TYRONE   I was trying to help.

JASON   That's what you call helping.

TYRONE   We had her man, we had her . . . With the bullshit.
With the shtick.

JASON   Yes. Yes we did. Then you had to go off with the nasty . . .

TYRONE   Women love that shit.

JASON   No they . . .

TYRONE   They do.

JASON   Shut up.

TYRONE   How do you think Timothy gets all the girls.

JASON   He's better looking.

TYRONE   Yeah . . . yeah that helps but just watch him. Watch him.

JASON   He's not very nice.

TYRONE   No he's not. He's not very nice and he's already had your
precious Jessica.

JASON   No he hasn't . . .

TYRONE   You sure?

JASON   I'll rip you in half again.

TYRONE   You try to so much as take me off your hand next time you
wake up it'll be with me stapled to your arm.

JASON   You wouldn't.

TYRONE   Look me in the eye and see if you believe that.

JASON   You wouldn . . .

TYRONE   I 100 per-fucking-cent would.

JASON   What do you want?

TYRONE   I want you to go back to the puppet club. I want you to get
up in front of the church. I want you to tell them all what assholes
they are. I want you to make Timmy bleed. I want you to fuck
Jessica. I want you to toughen the fuck up.

JASON   I don't want any of those things.

TYRONE   What do you want?

JASON I don't want to have to hurt anyone. I want to be kind and respectful to women. I want to care for my body and my mind.

TYRONE Jesus.

JASON I want to fall in love. I want happiness.

TYRONE You want to live in a fucking fairy tale.

JASON That's what Daddy did.

TYRONE That's bullshit. He couldn't hack it in college so he joined up.

JASON It was an important time in history.

TYRONE He came back and your mother carried his ass through school.

JASON That's how relationships work.

TYRONE He was miserable when you were born.

JASON Shut up.

TYRONE It's true.

JASON I can't . . .

TYRONE He was miserable. He got trapped. Then he ate until he had a fucking heart attack.

JASON Nononono.

TYRONE This is life.

JASON No it's not.

TYRONE Yes it is.

JASON There was love there.

TYRONE Did she leave you on the side of the road?

(*Beat.*)

JASON She's hurting.

TYRONE Yes or no?

JASON Yes.

TYRONE You tried to tell her you love her and she screamed.

JASON It's true.

TYRONE You want to make her happy.

JASON It's been for her.

TYRONE Yeah yeah I know, it's all for her. And look at you. Jesus you cry like a fat girl.

JASON I wanna go back to sleep.

TYRONE I know. But I won't let you.

JASON Why won't you let me?

TYRONE 'Cause we're all we got.

JASON But . . .

TYRONE No matter what they say. They will leave us. Hurt us. Scream and rage. It's you and me kid. Just you and me. Like a Saturday night.

JASON Who's on first.

TYRONE Right. So what do you say?

JASON I say . . . Okay.

ACT 1. SCENE 6.

We're back in the basement.

PASTOR GREG *enters.*

He is shocked by the state of the room.

PASTOR GREG   What the heck. What the heck. What the heck man.
   Oh come on. Son of a biscuit. God Bless America.

He goes to get his tools.

A hammer. A saw. A new poster of happy children, apparently he buys them in bulk.

The PASTOR *gets up on a ladder.*

He taps the light bulb.

MARGERY *come in.*

The bulb connects.

The stage gets brighter.

Things get a little weird.

MARGERY   Oh! Pastor! My my!

PASTOR GREG   Margery.

MARGERY   What a mess.

PASTOR GREG   Yeah.

JASON *enters.*

PASTOR GREG   Jason.

JASON Pastor.

PASTOR GREG Jason what happened to your little friend.

JASON I don't wanna . . .

TYRONE Spent the night outside. It was a hard night.

TYRONE *gives* PASTOR GREG *the shit eye.*

TYRONE Can I fill in anymore blanks for you?

PASTOR GREG You are getting . . . real good with that puppet.

JASON *yanks* TYRONE *away from the* PASTOR.

Corralling him to confer in the corner.

JASON Thank you sir.

PASTOR GREG Margey you gotta minute?

MARGERY No sir I do not. Sunday advances upon me wasted
minute by wasted minute.

PASTOR GREG Could you make the time.

MARGERY Listen Greg.

PASTOR GREG It isn't about that.

MARGERY Fine. What?

PASTOR GREG Did you leave the door unlocked last time you were
in here?

MARGERY I . . . I?

PASTOR GREG Who would do this? The bookshelf is knocked over.
Posters ripped to shreds. The sink in the bathroom is half knocked
off like someone was sitting on it . . . like they was bouncing up
and down on it . . . hard . . . real hard . . .

MARGERY No. Greg. I . . . I didn't . . . I locked the door.

PASTOR GREG I just can't figure it out.

TIMOTHY *almost runs in.*

TIMOTHY Hey.

PASTOR GREG Hello Timothy.

TIMOTHY How are you Mrs. Stevens?

MARGERY Fine. How are you?

TIMOTHY Pretty sweet. I've been thinking so much about ways to improve the puppet club. I have wanted so much to share them with you.

MARGERY Timothy, please take your seat.

PASTOR GREG Timothy where were you on Monday?

TIMOTHY I was here.

PASTOR GREG Don't lie to me son.

TIMOTHY I have no reason to lie sir.

PASTOR GREG I came by and there was no one here.

TIMOTHY I was late.

MARGERY He was late. We had a short conversation and then we both left. Isn't that right Timothy.

TIMOTHY Short but deep.

MARGERY Timothy.

TIMOTHY We had a conversation about my ideas for the puppet club. A conversation I would like to continue soon.

PASTOR GREG What's goin on here?

MARGERY Nothing.

PASTOR GREG Margery are you covering for Timothy?

MARGERY No Greg.

PASTOR GREG Because if this young man has vandalized church property—

MARGERY Timothy. We have to practice. Pastor, we can discuss this later.

PASTOR GREG I'll be watching you.

TIMOTHY I know. I've seen you outside the window while I shower.

MARGERY Timothy.

TIMOTHY It's really creepy.

PASTOR GREG I will pray for you son. Marge, I want to talk to you later.

MARGERY Yes Pastor.

The PASTOR *exits.*

MARGERY *opens up her bag, she gets out some books.*

TIM *sits next to* JASON.

TIMOTHY What's up dildo baby?

TYRONE (*To* JASON.) Come on, kid.

JASON I cain't.

TYRONE Ugh. (*To* TIMOTHY.) Hey. Do you know how easy it is to find someone's home address on the internet?

TIMOTHY What did you just say?

TYRONE Fun fact number two. The smallest of cuts to the Achilles' tendon will cripple a man for life.

TIMOTHY What the fuck?

TYRONE The calf muscle rolls up the leg like a flapping window shade.

TIMOTHY Today is not the day to fuck with me turd.

TYRONE What a shame cause I had oral surgery this afternoon and have not been able to indulge my sweet tooth.

TIMOTHY What does that mean?

JASON I have no idea.

TYRONE It means I'm about ready to eat your candy ass up.

MARGERY Boys we have to get to work.

TIMOTHY *for the first time clocks how strange what's going on actually is.*

TIMOTHY Yes Ma'am.

MARGERY So, Pastor Greg has asked us to perform before the congregation this Sunday. That means that because of Monday's poor attendance . . .

TIMOTHY I was here.

MARGERY I know Timothy.

TIMOTHY Just in case you forgot. In case you forgot. I was here. That did happen.

MARGERY Due to Monday's poor attendance we have something like four evenings to get something together. That is okay. I have been poring over the skit books and I think our best bet is to do some of the old stories. I'm not sure if the congregation is ready for either one of you to don a Jesus puppet and be nailed to a miniature cross.

TYRONE *laughs.*

MARGERY So we're gonna stick to the Old Testament. I was hoping we'd get Jessica so we could do the Temptation of Eve or Lot's wife but . . .

Of course at this point JESSICA *walks in.*

MARGERY Speak of the devil . . .

JESSICA I hope not.

MARGERY I am so glad to see you Jessie. Did your Mom get my message?

JESSICA I'm here.

MARGERY Okay. Sit down.

TIMOTHY Lesbian.

JESSICA So.

TIMOTHY So . . .

JESSICA Idiot. Ugggg. Hi Jason.

JASON Hi Jessie.

TYRONE You are the most beautiful thing I've ever seen.

JESSICA Jason what happened to Tyrone?

TYRONE This is what I am without you.

TYRONE *starts singing "You've Lost that Lovin' Feeling."*

MARGERY I'm gonna make some photocopies. Will you kids set up the stage while I'm gone?

TIMOTHY Do you need some help Mrs. Stevens?

MARGERY No Timothy. I need you to stay here and help the others.

TIMOTHY But . . . sharing . . .

MARGERY No buts Timothy. No buts and no sharing . . .

MARGERY *leaves.*

JASON *wrestles with a singing* TYRONE.

JESSICA *starts to put up the stage.*

TIMOTHY *just stares off after* MARGERY.

JESSICA So Timmy you just gonna sit there all night or you gonna help us put up this stage.

TIMOTHY So Jesse are you gonna just stand there with your milk stink vagina or are you gonna wash it at some point.

TYRONE You don't talk to her like that.

TIMOTHY What?

TYRONE *pulls at* JASON'*s collar.*

JASON *reluctantly enters the fray.*

JASON Tyrone is right Timothy. The way you talk to Jessica is unacceptable.

JESSICA Don't bother with him Jason. He's not worth it.

TIMOTHY I'm not worth it. You're not worth it. And I'm getting tired of this little retard's Dr. Jekyll and Miss Piggy Act.

TYRONE What did you just call me?

JESSICA Seriously Jason.

TYRONE *dismisses* JESSICA *with a noise or two.*

TYRONE Did you just call me Miss Piggy?

TIMOTHY Jason you have serious problems.

JESSICA Jason, I get it. It's sweet.

JASON I'm not trying to be sweet.

TYRONE Don't look at the kid asshole look at me.

TIMOTHY Jason, I am not going to talk to your puppet.

TYRONE Look at the kid and tell me who you think is in control.

TIMOTHY This is pretty fucking weird man I'm gonna get your mom.

TYRONE Is that how is works you little dick piece of shit. You push around girls and boys that are smaller than you. You talk big and nasty. You blow hard. You puff yourself up and wear black. You posture. You pose. You're nothing but shit and wind. The moment somebody calls you out you run like a scared little bitch. So run. Run. Take your tiny shriveled dick and run. 'Cause everybody in this room knows exactly what you are. Nothing.

JESSICA Jason what is going on?

JASON I don't know.

TIMOTHY Nothing. Oh yeah?

TYRONE Yeah.

TIMOTHY Say whatever you want. I know I'm something.

TYRONE What are you?

TIMOTHY Enough for your mother.

JASON What?

TIMOTHY You heard me. I fucked your mother.

TYRONE *starts to laugh.*

JESSICA Jason.

TIMOTHY I fucked your mother and she liked it.

TYRONE*'s laugh gets scary.*

JESSICA Jason.

TIMOTHY She liked it a lot.

TYRONE*'s laugh is terrifying.*

JESSICA Please stop.

TYRONE *stops.*

Looks at her.

TYRONE Okay.

TYRONE *looks back at* TIMOTHY.

He smiles.

TIMOTHY What?

TYRONE Just thinking about what you'll look like without an ear.

TYRONE *flies at* TIMOTHY.

JESSICA *screams.*

JASON NONONONONONONO.

TYRONE *bites off* TIMOTHY*'s ear.*

MARGERY *runs back on with her copies.*

MARGERY Jason.

JASON *comes up blood on his face.*

TYRONE *follows after ear in his mouth.*

TYRONE Did you?

MARGERY *shoots an unintentional look at* TIMOTHY.

MARGERY Jason?

TYRONE You did.

PASTOR GREG *comes on.*

PASTOR GREG Can you kids hold it . . . is that blood?

TIMOTHY Yes, you dipshit.

TYRONE How could you?

MARGERY I don't know what you're talking about.

TYRONE You can lie to them but you can't lie to me.

MARGERY Jason . . .

TYRONE I know what you are.

PASTOR GREG What is he talking about?

TIMOTHY He's crazy.

TYRONE He's a child.

TIMOTHY He's possessed.

PASTOR GREG Who's a child.

TIMOTHY He's fucking demonic.

TYRONE How could you fuck a ch . . .

MARGERY Timothy's right. The devil's got him.

TYRONE The devil. You want the devil? I'll give you the devil.

TYRONE *loses his shit.*

Everyone stands struck.

At the height of his tantrum DEMONIC THE PUPPET *makes an awful noise and the light bulb bursts.*

Everybody screams and runs to the door.

'Cept MARGERY.

MARGERY Jason . . .

PASTOR GREG Margery come on.

PASTOR GREG *pulls her out the door with the rest.*

TYRONE That went well.

End of Act 1.

So that happened . . .

ACT 2. SCENE 1.

Now we're next door.

The four of them are sitting in the PASTOR*'s office.*

There's a bottle of rum and a puppet repair kit on the table.

Lights up MARGERY *is tending to* TIMOTHY*'s ear. Pulling through it, sewing it on with puppet thread or what not.*

TIM *yowls.*

JESSICA *is watching it all with her hands in her pockets as* PASTOR GREG *is digging through a thick book or perhaps trawling the Internet.*

TIM *yowls again.*

MARGERY Bite down!

PASTOR GREG Margery that's a lot of blood.

MARGERY Problem one solved. Ear stays on.

She pulls at it.

TIMMY *makes a confused noise halfway between pain and pleasure.*

MARGERY Now what about Jason.

PASTOR GREG Ummm.

JESSICA Well who bought him the puppet with teeth?

MARGERY This isn't funny Jessie.

JESSICA I'm not trying to be funny. My puppet doesn't have teeth.

MARGERY Your puppet isn't possessed by the devil.

JESSICA Is it the puppet that's possessed or Jason?

MARGERY Jessica.

PASTOR GREG That is an interesting question.

MARGERY I have had enough interesting questions for one day. The devil is in that puppet and we are goin to exorcise him right out and have everyone back home by midnight. That's what I want and that's what Jesus wants and that's what's gonna happen. Right?

Nobody answers.

JESSICA Do Lutherans even do exorcisms?

PASTOR GREG Strangely enough yes. After the Reformation when the church split it was still a pretty popular service. It just isn't done much anymore.

MARGERY See? Okay? Here we go.

JESSICA Do you really think this is the best way to deal with all this?

MARGERY Do you have any other suggestions?

JESSICA I don't know 911?

MARGERY Yes officer my underage son's puppet just bit off his friend's ear. Who can we call? Who? Who you gonna call?

TIMOTHY Ghostbusters?

TIMOTHY *laughs.*

MARGERY *douses his ear with the rum.*

He yowls again.

JESSICA This is crazy. We need help.

PASTOR GREG Margey I can't help but . . .

MARGERY Why don't you kids go get a coke.

JESSICA Really?

MARGERY Yeah you'll feel better.

TIMOTHY I feel awesome right now.

MARGERY Pastor Greg could use some quiet to concentrate on his pre-exorcism prep.

PASTOR GREG Actually I have remarkable powers of concentration.

MARGERY Timmy could use something cold to put on his ear.

JESSICA Then why don't we get ice instead of a coke.

MARGERY Brilliant Jessica. Brilliant. By all means you f-ing genius get ice and not a coke. Just give us a moment in this office alone.

JESSICA Ummm . . . okay. Come on Tim.

TIMOTHY I don't wanna go.

MARGERY Please Tim.

TIMOTHY For you.

JESSICA Jesus.

JESSICA *drags* TIMOTHY *out.*

The two of them look at each other.

MARGERY Greg we can't. No police . . . we can't. We just can't.

PASTOR GREG Margery calm down.

MARGERY They'll take him away.

PASTOR GREG Maybe he needs to be taken away.

MARGERY No. No. I can't. I can't lose him too.

PASTOR GREG I know.

He goes to his book shelf and grabs a Bible.

PASTOR GREG Ok. Then I guess that leaves just me.

MARGERY Well what are you gonna do?

PASTOR GREG I have no idea. I guess I'm just gonna try to talk to him.

MARGERY Who knows what he might say. He's out of his mind. He might say any kind of filthy thing . . .

PASTOR GREG That's a risk I have to take.

GREG *leaves and she stays there.*

Nothing to do but take a pull off of that bottle.

ACT 2. SCENE 2.

So the basement is a little bit of a wreck.

JASON *and* TYRONE *have redecorated, aggressively. Crucified Barbies. Behead stuffed bears. Written filthy things on the walls with poster paint.*

JASON Why'd you have to tell 'em you were the devil?

TYRONE I didn't. They called me that first.

JASON Yeah but you didn't tell 'em no.

TYRONE No, no I didn't.

JASON Are you the devil?

TYRONE Are you?

JASON I don't know. I don't think so.

TYRONE Do you think devilish thoughts?

JASON Uhhh.

TYRONE Lemme get that one for you. Yes. Yes you do.

JASON But I ain't done 'em.

TYRONE No you haven't and what do you have to show for it.

JASON My mother loves me.

TYRONE Looks like you aren't the only one getting your mother's sweet love, HEY-O.

JASON That's not funny.

TYRONE No it's not. What is she saying to you when you tells you to behave. When she says sit down. Stay still. She is saying stay small. Be less. Be little. Which was fine when you were a child. But what about now? Who can you count on now?

JASON I don't know.

TYRONE Who gives you want you want?

JASON I don't know.

TYRONE Yes you do.

JASON I don't want to be bad.

TYRONE Yes you do.

JASON How did you break the light bulb?

TYRONE I didn't. You did.

There is the sound of keys in the door.

JASON Oh god it's the police.

TYRONE No it's not.

JASON We're gonna be in trouble.

TYRONE No we're not. You don't get it. We are the trouble.

The door cracks open a bit.

PASTOR GREG (*Offstage.*) Hello.

JASON Hi Pastor Greg.

PASTOR GREG *comes in.*

PASTOR GREG Thank God Jason . . .

TYRONE Welcome to Hell . . .

A heating pipe might crack a bit sending steam into the room. A door might slam. A bird might crash into the window.

PASTOR GREG Holy.

TYRONE Leave or prepare to forfeit your mortal soul.

PASTOR GREG Jason I wanna talk to you.

JASON Okay.

TYRONE No not okay. Fall down. Fall down on your knees . . . mortal . . .

PASTOR GREG Jason could you get him to stop with . . .

JASON Just ignore him. It's fine.

TYRONE Fine? It is not fine. It's evil. This is the very moment you
surrender your soul to your dark lord.

PASTOR GREG Shut up Tyrone.

TYRONE What you do not fear my power?

PASTOR GREG Is that all? Maybe you did take off a piece of that
kid's ear, but if all you got is popping bulbs and slamming doors,
I think I can take down a puppet on the hand of an unathletic
child.

TYRONE I'ma gonna . . . I'm gonna . . .

PASTOR GREG What?

TYRONE I'm gonna think about what to do next.

TYRONE *thinks.*

JASON Isn't there supposed to be a young priest and an old priest.

PASTOR GREG We aren't Catholics Jason. It's not as simple as
blaming everything on possession.

TYRONE Oh he's possessed all right.

PASTOR GREG Jason.

TYRONE What if I make the walls bleed.

PASTOR GREG Go ahead. I need to repaint anyway.

TYRONE *goes behind the puppet theater.*

JASON How do we determine if I'm possessed.

PASTOR GREG We should take you to see someone. Find out if
this isn't a symptom of something . . . something else.

JASON So why don't you call a doctor.

PASTOR GREG Your mother doesn't want us too.

JASON Why?

PASTOR GREG Well kiddo you and your friend here bit off
Timothy's ear.

JASON It was just the lobe.

PASTOR GREG That's criminal and with an evil puppet on your hand I don't think you're going to regular kid jail. You'll probably go to special kid jail.

JASON Oh no.

TYRONE *spins around starts to listen.*

PASTOR GREG And I think we can deal with this right here. I know you need someone right now. I'd like to be that someone if you'll let me.

JASON *looks at* TYRONE.

PASTOR GREG Jason your father was an unhappy man.
I tried to help him. He was hungry but for the wrong things. And I like to think I helped your mother. I like to think that I am a beacon for her. Helping her find her way back to waiting arms . . . the waiting arms . . . of the church.

TYRONE You love her.

PASTOR GREG What?

TYRONE The kid's mother. You are balls deep in love.

PASTOR GREG I respect her as a dutiful Christian woman.

TYRONE Bullshit. One of the marks of possession is secret knowledge.

PASTOR GREG How do you know that?

TYRONE Lemme say it again. One of the marks of possession is secret knowledge.

PASTOR GREG Also knowledge of an unexposed foreign tongue.

TYRONE Well pardon my french asshole but Margey fucked lil' Tim-Tim.

PASTOR GREG *gets up.*

PASTOR GREG Jason, what?

TYRONE You heard me.

PASTOR GREG That's a lie.

TYRONE They fucked all over the place. Probably here. Probably
   there. Probably in your shitty little church.

PASTOR GREG *takes* TYRONE *by the throat and* JASON *by the wrist.*

PASTOR GREG You're a lying demon.

TYRONE Oh now I'm a demon . . . secret knowledge.

PASTOR GREG Gimme that stupid sock. Gimme that fucking sock.

JASON Pastor please.

TYRONE Tell him.

JASON It's not a secret. Timothy told us.

The PASTOR *freezes.*

PASTOR GREG Timothy is a . . .

TYRONE But look at your face. You know. You totally know. They're
   probably fucking right now.

PASTOR GREG I . . .

JASON Pastor it hurts!

The PASTOR *drops the kid's hand.*

TYRONE Fuck with me will you.

PASTOR GREG I have to go. I have to leave. I have to go now.

JASON Pastor, Pastor don't . . .

PASTOR GREG *walks the fuck out.*

JASON *looks at his* PUPPET. *Who is clearly pleased with himself.*

JASON What do we do now?

TYRONE Wait. She'll be back.

The PASTOR *locks the door behind him.*

ACT 2. SCENE 3.

So MARGERY *is alone in the* PASTOR*'s office.*

There's a bobblehead Jesus on his desk. She pokes it. It bobbles.

She takes a nip of the bottle on the PASTOR*'s desk.*

TIMMY *comes in.*

MARGERY   Hello.

TIMOTHY   Hey.

(*Beat.*)

MARGERY   This is . . .

TIMOTHY   This is what? Were you going to say wrong?

MARGERY   This is making everyone crazy.

TIMOTHY   But . . . I love you.

MARGERY   You love me.

She's getting angry.

TIMOTHY   I love you.

MARGERY   You fucking love me?

TIMOTHY   I said it twice. Well three times if you count . . .

MARGERY   You know what love is like?

TIMOTHY   Nice I think. You go to brunch . . .

MARGERY   Love is a day to day pile of shit.

TIMOTHY   That's very poeti . . .

She grabs his balls.

TIMOTHY   OOOOOOOOOH.

MARGERY Is this nice?

TIMOTHY Kinda . . .

MARGERY Is this?

She twists.

He makes a guttural sound.

MARGERY That's what love is like.

She throws him off.

He hits the floor.

MARGERY Is that what you want?

He looks at her.

He gets up off the ground.

MARGERY What?

There's a stare down.

MARGERY What?

She breaks it with violence.

TIMOTHY Yeah.

Things are getting hectic.

TIMOTHY Give it to me.

She socks him.

TIMOTHY That all you got?

MARGERY No.

She rushes him.

MARGERY This is the last time.

TIMOTHY Whatever you say.

She grabs his head.

MARGERY I mean it.

TIMOTHY Okay.

MARGERY *pushes his head down her body.*

JESSICA *walks in.*

JESSICA Mrs. Stevens.

MARGERY Jessica!

They break apart.

JESSICA Hey guys.

TIMOTHY Jessica get the fuck out.

JESSICA I'm going to. Mrs. Stevens, can I get the keys to your
 mini van? I need the puppet supplies.

MARGERY Take the keys. Take anything you want.

She tries to hand JESSICA *her purse.*

TIMOTHY *intercepts the bag.*

TIMOTHY Oh I will.

He tosses the thing to JESSICA *and advances on* MARGERY.

JESSICA Oh my God.

TIMOTHY Take the fucking purse.

MARGERY Take it all.

MARGERY *throws herself at* TIMOTHY.

MARGERY I don't give a shit anymore take it all.

JESSICA Are you fucking kidding me?

TIMOTHY Go.

JESSICA Gahhh.

JESSICA *leaves.* TIMOTHY *locks the door and turns.*

TIMOTHY Oh you nasty bitch.

MARGERY I am. I am a nasty bitch.

TIMOTHY You teasing tricksy little slut. You've been driving me crazy all week.

MARGERY Say it in my ear.

TIMOTHY I've blistered my dick thinking about you.

MARGERY Tell me about it.

TIMOTHY I found your picture in the church directory and . . .

A knock at the door.

MARGERY Jessica go away. Timothy.

TIMOTHY Jessica, please. You don't wanna be in here for this.

PASTOR GREG This isn't Jessica. Open this door.

MARGERY Oh shit.

TIMOTHY Be brave my dove. It is time he discovered our love.

TIMOTHY *goes to hold her around the waist.*

MARGERY What are you doing?

PASTOR GREG I'm coming in.

MARGERY No Pastor.

TIMOTHY Do it.

TIMOTHY *shuts her up with a kiss.*

PASTOR GREG *opens the door.*

There is a little pause.

PASTOR GREG I can't believe it.

MARGERY Pastor . . .

TIMOTHY Believe it.

MARGERY Timmy let go.

PASTOR GREG Let her go.

TIMOTHY No she likes this.

PASTOR GREG Stop.

TIMOTHY Get Off.

MARGERY Timothy.

TIMOTHY Honey.

MARGERY Don't call me honey.

TIMOTHY Sweetheart.

MARGERY Mrs. Stevens.

TIMOTHY What are you doing? You . . . you're my world.

MARGERY Timothy you're a child.

TIMOTHY No. I'm not.

PASTOR GREG Timothy.

TIMOTHY I'm not. Why would you do this to me?

PASTOR GREG Tim please.

TIMOTHY Why would you play with my feelings. You. You bitch.

MARGERY Hey now.

PASTOR GREG Timothy stop.

TIMOTHY No. Gaaaah.

TIMOTHY *throws over the chair.*

PASTOR GREG *snaps and rushes at him pinning him to the wall.*

PASTOR GREG Listen here. You don't break other people's things.
  You don't talk to women that way. You don't do everything that
  comes into your mind.

TIMOTHY You can't tell me what to do.

PASTOR GREG No I can't. But I can beat the shit out of you.
  Believe that.

TIMOTHY Mrs. Stevens.

PASTOR GREG I've wanted to teach you a lesson for a good ·
  long while . . . but I haven't. 'Cause that's not how you act.
  'Cause I know how to act. 'Cause I'm grown.

He looks at MARGERY.

PASTOR GREG 'Cause I know better.

PASTOR GREG *drops the kid.*

PASTOR GREG Now pull up your pants and go home.

TIMOTHY No. You can't.

PASTOR GREG I said go home.

TIMOTHY I'll tell. I'll tell on you.

PASTOR GREG Go do it.

TIMOTHY Mrs. Stevens . . .

MARGERY Really Tim you should go.

TIMOTHY But I love you . . . you bitch.

MARGERY I'm sorry Tim.

TIMOTHY Not as sorry as you're gonna be.

He runs off.

There is a silence in the room.

MARGERY I'm sorry.

PASTOR GREG Me too Margery.

MARGERY I was . . . I am confused.

PASTOR GREG That's great. I am not.

MARGERY What are you talking about?

PASTOR GREG I have to call the police Margery.

MARGERY No . . .

PASTOR GREG No? No? I . . . uh . . . there's no more no. I can't
have you around. You can't be around if this. If this is what you're
gonna do. If this is what you are.

MARGERY What I am?

PASTOR GREG Yes.

MARGERY What I am?

PASTOR GREG Margery . . .

MARGERY What am I Greg . . .

PASTOR GREG I don't know.

MARGERY No you don't. No you fucking. Don't. I'll tell you what I am. I am disappointed.

PASTOR GREG Disappointed?

MARGERY I am let down. I am failed.

PASTOR GREG Failed by who Margery.

MARGERY By you. By all of you.

PASTOR GREG Tell me about it Marg.

MARGERY You're a real piece of shit Pastor Greg. I have endured some pussy pasty limp dick come-ons in my time but really? My arms were made to hold you.

PASTOR GREG I have feelings too, Marge. I have human feelings.

MARGERY La-di-fucking da.

PASTOR GREG You wanted to talk. I listened. You needed a place to go I was here. You needed work for idle hand. I gave you puppets . . .

MARGERY Oh and you think that entitles you to a piece of this.

PASTOR GREG You brought an abomination into the house of God.

MARGERY You used the church to try and fuck me.

(*Beat.*)

PASTOR GREG That isn't fair, Marge.

MARGERY No no. Not fair is being taken advantage of. Not fair is being abandoned by your husband. Not fair is having a kid that won't give you one . . . the one thing you ask for. Just be there for Momma. Just be there for Momma and don't talk to your fucking puppet.

PASTOR GREG He's having a hard time.

MARGERY Stop making excuses. No more excuses. He's having a hard time. I'm sad, I need a Whopper. I'm too busy to go to the doctor. Excuses. Fucking excuses. Fucking bullshit.

She sees a Bible.

MARGERY Fucking Jesus.

She pulls the Bible off the shelf.

PASTOR GREG Give that to me.

He tries to take it from her.

MARGERY Fucking wisdom of the ages. Fucking stories. And fucking rules and fucking Geneology.

MARGERY Abraham begat Issac.

She tears a page out of the Bible.

PASTOR GREG Stop it Marg.

He steps towards her.

MARGERY Issac begat Dorkus.

She dodges him. Shredding the old book as she moves.

PASTOR GREG Margery give it to me.

MARGERY Dorkus begat Gibberish. Gibberish begat balderdash.

PASTOR GREG You know what go ahead.

MARGERY Stupid fucking God.

PASTOR GREG Go on. Keep going, if this is what helps.

In frustration she throws the tattered Bible on the floor.

MARGERY None of it helps. I touched that stupid boy. I made my son crazy. Everything I touch turns to shit.

PASTOR GREG Then what now.

She crumples.

MARGERY Take me away. I cain't touch anything else. I don't wanna hurt anybody else. Call the police.

PASTOR GREG Maybe.

MARGERY Maybe?

MARGERY *sniffles a little.*

GREG *goes over and helps her up.*

PASTOR GREG First things first.

ACT 2. SCENE 4.

We're back in basement.

JASON *is messing with door.*

He's got one of PASTOR GREG'*s screwdrivers out of the tool box.*

JASON I want a frozen yogurt.

TYRONE *gives him the shit eye.*

TYRONE The fuck?

JASON Mom and I go to TCBY after puppet practice. If I had frozen
yogurt right now it would mean everything is fine.

TYRONE I won't buy it. I know you're hungry. I know you're twitchy
and angry and you want everything in the world. Every single
goddamned thing. Why don't you just admit it and we can get
some shit done.

JASON I want out of this basement.

TYRONE You don't want out of this basement you want everyone
on the other side worrying. You want them to understand that you
hurt, that you are angry at her.

JASON No.

TYRONE You just can't tell them.

At this moment a high tight basement window opens up.

JASON They called in the feds.

Instead of the FBI . . .

It's a LADY PUPPET.

You might remember JOLENE *from earlier, but she's undergone a bit of a transformation.*

She is now sexy, very very sexy, the kind of blunt sexy that is appealing to the inexperienced or the young or businessmen at a conference in Atlanta.

JOLENE Drop your cocks boys. Company's a coming.

TYRONE Hell yes. This sausage fest is officially over!

Tumbling through the window a little coltish is of course JESSICA.

JESSICA Hi.

JASON Hi. What are you doing here?

JOLENE I heard there was a bad boy here. I heard he was real bad. You bad, boy?

TYRONE Girl. I have everything you need.

JOLENE Come on big talker let's get this done.

They move the puppets close to one another.

TYRONE *is not as aggressive as he promised.*

He begins to sing to her, something like "Hello" by Mr. Lionel Ritchie.

JOLENE Hey. You nervous.

TYRONE Am I nervous? Yeah. I mean . . . you know . . . just a little.

She puts a hand on his puppet chest.

JOLENE Relax. Just breathe.

He does. He drops his head.

She moves down his puppet body.

TYRONE I'm . . .

JOLENE What?

TYRONE It's my first time.

JOLENE I know.

She might reach up under the place where JASON*'s hand enters the* PUPPET.

TYRONE *might gasp.*

JOLENE Just leave everything to me.

TYRONE Wait . . . wait. . . .

TYRONE *reaches his head around and looks at* JASON *and* JESSICA.

TYRONE I want y'all to know I know what's going on here.

JESSICA *and* JASON *look at each other confused.*

JASON I . . . I don't . . .

JESSICA What do you mean?

TYRONE I've seen Bugs Bunny, mutherfucker. I know what's going down. It's just . . .

JOLENE Don't look at them. Look at me.

JOLENE *lifts her top.* JESSICA *has paid great attention to detail.* JOLENE *has nipples made out of buttons.*

TYRONE It's just too good. Even if it ain't real.

TYRONE *goes in for a real open mouth no holds barred kiss.*

JESSICA *and* JASON *look at each other awkwardly while their puppets get further and further along.*

JASON Thanks.

JESSICA No problem.

TYRONE*'s getting into it.*

TYRONE *checks in with* JOLENE.

TYRONE Is this okay? Are you. Are you ready?

JOLENE So ready.

TYRONE *mounts* JOLENE.

JESSICA How long do you think this is gonna go on?

JASON Well he said it was his first time so probably not too long.

JESSICA I didn't mean that. I meant this. All of this

JASON You meant . . .

JESSICA The whole . . .

She gestures to him and the puppet and the puppet sex.

JESSICA This whole thing.

JASON Well it's just . . . new. As long as we keep him . . . occupied, I think everything will be fine.

JESSICA Jason, that is scary.

JASON I thought that's what you girls liked.

JESSICA Who is you girls?

JASON You. The kind of girls that are into Timothy.

JESSICA Sometimes.

TYRONE Jessus. Jeeesuuusss. Oh my god.

JASON *looks away disappointed.*

JESSICA But just sometimes. I also like "Who's on first?" Although it was more impressive before I knew your hand was possessed.

JASON I know. I just wish I believed you.

JESSICA About what?

JASON People say this stuff. All this stuff about what you can be. Who you should be. Being yourself and shit and I don't buy it. They don't act that way. Nice never got me anything. It makes me feel . . . like . . . like . . .

JESSICA Like you're not enough?

JASON Yeah.

JESSICA You don't have to be Timmy. You don't have to be

Tyrone. You're right. A little of it is nice. But you realize that you don't have to go all the way, right? You realize that you can be your own person.

JASON But I don't know what that is.

JESSICA What do you want it to be?

JASON I don't know.

JESSICA 'Cause I will tell you right now, we can't go to the home-coming dance as long as you have that thing on your arm.

TYRONE HOOOOOMEECUUUUUMMMMMINGGGGGGGGGG.

TYRONE *collapses in a heap on top of the* FEMALE PUPPET.

JESSICA Let me rephrase that. Do you want to be a shallow violent foul-mouthed puppet for the rest of your life? Think about it.

The locks on the door make their clattering noise.

The door comes open and it's PASTOR GREG *and* MARGERY.

PASTOR GREG Jessica are you okay? What are you doing in here?

JESSICA Puppet practice.

TYRONE *for some reason is limp.*

JASON *stares at his* PUPPET.

JESSICA Think about Homecoming, okay Jason?

JASON Okay. You too.

JESSICA Good night, everyone.

She walks out the door.

JASON *is studying* TYRONE.

PASTOR GREG Jason, your Mother has something she'd like to say. Margery?

TYRONE *comes roaring back to life.*

TYRONE (*Coughs.*) Bitch.

PASTOR GREG Tyrone, I will not have . . .

MARGERY Greg please. Jason . . .

TYRONE Talk to me. You're talking to me. I can smell him on you.

MARGERY I know what I did was wrong. I understand that it can't be easy going through what you are going through. And I want you to know it isn't easy for me either.

TYRONE It actually seems real easy for you. Seems like you just do whatever the fuck you want.

MARGERY That . . . that is . . . I am lost. I am hurt.

TYRONE Oh wow.

MARGERY Jason you can't do this. I need . . .

TYRONE Oh tell us more about what you need.

MARGERY We. I mean we. We can't keep going like this. We can't pretend everything is okay. We can't . . .

TYRONE Chain the old man. Make him so miserable he eats himself to death. Can't kill my father . . .

JASON *looks at the* PUPPET.

JASON our . . .

The PUPPET *looks at* JASON.

JASON I . . .

JASON *looks at his* MOTHER.

MARGERY Jason.

JASON Why didn't you help him?

MARGERY I tried.

JASON You failed. You . . . why didn't you take care of him?

MARGERY He just . . . your father had problems . . .

JASON So it's his fault.

PASTOR GREG It's nobody's fault . . .

JASON Nobody's fault? Nobody's fault.

PASTOR GREG Jason son forgiveness is . . .

PASTOR GREG *tries to come in between them.*

TYRONE *comes back with a vengeance.*

JASON Don't fucking touch me.

MARGERY Baby no. Let me explain.

JASON Mom, stop fucking crying.

PASTOR GREG Jason please.

JASON Fuck you.

MARGERY Just talk to me.

JASON You're poison. Get the fuck out.

TYRONE Yeah. Get the fuck out.

She runs out of the room.

JASON Mom.

TYRONE Let her go.

PASTOR GREG *shakes his head.*

PASTOR GREG Are you happy now?

TYRONE Jason is fucking ecstatic.

PASTOR GREG Jason are you happy? I don't think you are.

TYRONE Don't you fucking contradict me.

TYRONE *pulls at the end of* JASON*'s arm. Like it's the* end of a dog's
lead chain.

PASTOR GREG Son, I think you are scared and confused and you
    know what. So am I. Everybody is struggling. A man has one
    voice Jason. And we gotta take responsibility for that. And that's
    the truth son.

TYRONE I'll give you the truth. You're a pussy. You're a fucking pussy.

PASTOR GREG You have to decide who comes out of this room. You. Or that. Take whatever time you need.

PASTOR GREG *leaves.*

TYRONE What an asshole. Can you believe that guy?

JASON *doesn't say anything.*

TYRONE I said can you believe that guy?

JASON Tyrone. I don't want to be your friend anymore.

TYRONE What? Are you kidding me?

JASON No I'm not kidding you. I want you to go away.

TYRONE We are about to have so much fun. We are right on the edge. Right on the cusp. There is great fun right around the corner. You wanna break the light bulb again? You liked that didn't you?

JASON No. No. I want you to go away.

TYRONE Well fuck you then. After all I . . . Jesus you got the girl didn't you. You told the bitch where to go. I . . . after all I have done.

JASON I'm sorry it took you.

TYRONE No. No. You will regret this.

JASON Never.

There is a stare off.

TYRONE Don't.

JASON Get ready.

TYRONE No.

JASON I'm taking you off.

TYRONE *sighs.*

TYRONE I guess you're right. We had a good run though didn't we?

JASON No. It was awful. Truly awful.

TYRONE High five.

JASON Why would I high five you for that?

TYRONE 'Cause I'll probably never see you again.

JASON *sighs.*

He goes up for a high five.

TYRONE *bites his finger.*

JASON Leggo.

TYRONE (*Through muffles.*) Fuck you.

JASON *pulls as hard as he can.*

JASON Ahhhhh.

TYRONE (*Through muffles.*) I'll pull it off you son of a bitch.

JASON *head butts the* PUPPET.

TYRONE *lets go.*

JASON *looks at his bloody bitten finger.*

JASON I can see bone.

TYRONE Might be the last thing you see.

TYRONE *goes for* JASON*'s throat.*

JASON AAAARRGGHHHH.

TYRONE You didn't think it'd be easy, did you?

JASON No. No. No.

JASON *slips his hand up under* TYRONE*'s shirt.*

TYRONE You'll never be rid of me.

JASON *slips the* PUPPET *right off.*

It falls to the floor.

JASON Jesus.

JASON *takes a deep breath. He walks over to* PASTOR GREG*'s tool box.*

He reaches in and gets one of the shop towels.

He wipes the blood off of his face and hands.

In the process his left hand becomes covered by the cloth and. . .

TYRONE *appears in the hand covered cloth.*

TYRONE NEVER.

JASON *sees* PASTOR GREG*'s hammer.*

JASON Oh yeah?

TYRONE You can't beat me.

JASON I don't have to beat you. Just shut you the fuck up.

JASON *raises the hammer high.*

He brings the hammer down on his cloth covered hand.

TYRONE Fuck you.

JASON No fuck you.

JASON *raises the hammer again.*

TYRONE Noooooo.

JASON Yes.

JASON *brings the hammer up again.*

He turns it over.

Claw side. Hesitates.

MARGERY *runs in.*

MARGERY Jason, what on earth . . . Jason.

She stops.

JASON Momma get out.

MARGERY Jason no.

JASON Momma I have to.

MARGERY No baby no.

He brings it up.

MARGERY *tries to grab the hammer.*

He brings it down.

She knocks his hand aside.

The hammer slams into her hand.

She screams.

JASON NO.

She stifles it.

JASON Oh my God Momma. Why . . . did you . . .

MARGERY Just . . . just . . .

Together they pull the hammer out of her flesh.

JASON WHA . . .

MARGERY BAAAAAAA.

JASON WHY.

MARGERY HUH.

He drops the hammer.

The PASTOR *runs in.*

PASTOR GREG Oh my God.

He sees MARGERY *with her hand all abloodied.*

He goes to her.

PASTOR GREG Margery

MARGERY No, don't.

PASTOR GREG We gotta get you to the hospital.

He sees JASON *clearly for the first time.*

PASTOR GREG Jason oh my god

GREG *starts to go to the boy.*

JASON *retreats.*

JASON LEAVE ME ALONE.

PASTOR GREG Jason.

JASON LEAVE ME THE FUCK ALONE.

His rage stuns the two of them.

MARGERY Go Greg.

GREG *doesn't move.*

MARGERY Go get the car. Bring it around front.

He hesitates.

PASTOR GREG But . . .

MARGERY Do it Greg. Now.

He does.

She pulls herself together. Fighting with the pain.

MARGERY Jason we gotta . . .

JASON I fucked it up. I fucked it all up. I hurt you.

MARGERY Jason.

He sinks to the floor.

JASON Just leave me alone.

MARGERY I will not.

He sinks to the floor.

She goes to him.

MARGERY   Now give me your hand.

She grabs the shop towel.

JASON   No, what if he comes back?

MARGERY   Then tell me, and I will try to listen.

He looks at his hand.

She takes a hold of it wrapping it in the towel.

JASON *exclaims in pain.*

MARGERY   Put pressure. Put pressure. Hold it up.

JASON   Jesus. Jesus.

MARGERY   Jason, baby.

They hold each other.

We hear a car pull up outside and headlights flash through the basement windows

MARGERY   Let's go get us some help.

They leave together.

As the lights fade we see the PUPPET *still on the floor grinning strangely.*

Darkness.

EPILOGUE

A flash of lightning.

A rumble of thunder.

From somewhere TYRONE *returns.*

Larger this time.

TYRONE Miss me? That's the thing about the devil. You need him.
Then you need him to go the fuck away. So some forsaken genius
started killing sheep. Lambs. Babies. Holding them up and saying
the devil in me is in this and this is dead. Then some body said
listen we're wasting a lot of sheep why don't we just kill the
sweetest guy we know. And that's how we invented Jesus. And so
for the last couple thousand years, merrily we roll along. Solving
our problems by putting horns on them and then watching our
saviors burn. Laugh, motherfuckers, that shit's funny. Maybe
someday we won't need that puppet show anymore. Maybe
someday we'll be able let ourselves off the hook for everything
we've always done and have always needed to do. But I doubt it.
Thing about a savior is you never know where to look. Might just
be the place you saw the devil before.

End of Play.